Popular Music Theory

Grade Five

by

Camilla Sheldon & Tony Skinner

A CIP record for this publication is available from the British Library.

ISBN: 1-898466-45-9

First edition © 2001 Registry Publications Ltd.

Published in Great Britain by

Registry House, Churchill Mews, Dennett Rd, Croydon, Surrey, CR0 3JH

Typesetting by

Take Note Publishing Limited, Lingfield, Surrey

Instrument photographs supplied by John Hornby Skewes Ltd. and Yamaha (UK) Ltd.

Printed in Great Britain by MFP, Manchester.

Contents

Introduction

This book covers the new material you need to know to take the London College of Music Grade Five examination in Popular Music Theory. Each chapter outlines the facts you need to know for the examination, together with the theory behind the facts. Each chapter is completed with some examples of the types of questions that will appear in the examination paper. The sample questions are intended to provide a clear guide as to the kind of questions that may be asked in the examination, however the list of questions is neither exclusive nor exhaustive. Once you've worked through the questions at the end of each section, you can check your answers by looking at the 'sample answers' in the back of the book.

As the requirements for each examination are cumulative, it is essential that you have a knowledge of the requirements for the previous grades. If you are not already familiar with this earlier material, it is recommended that you study the preceding books in this series.

musical terms

Sometimes there are two different names that can be used for the same musical elements. Also, the terminology that is widely used in N. America (and increasingly amongst pop, rock and jazz musicians in the U.K. and elsewhere) is different to that traditionally used in the U.K. and other parts of Europe.

A summary of the main alternative terms is shown below. In the examination you can use either version. In this book we generally use the terms shown in the left-hand column, as these are the ones that are more commonly used amongst popular music musicians.

whole note	=	semibreve
half note	=	minim
quarter note	=	crotchet
eighth note	=	quaver
sixteenth note	=	semiquaver
whole step	=	whole tone
half step	=	semitone
staff	=	stave
treble clef	=	G clef
bass clef	=	F clef
measures	=	bars
keynote	=	tonic
leger line	=	ledger line
flat 3rd, 6th or 7th	=	minor 3rd, 6th or 7th
flat 5th	=	diminished 5th
sharp 5th	=	augmented 5th

Section One – scales and keys

In this section of the exam you may be asked to write out and identify any of the following scales (and their key signatures).

Scales with key signatures to the range of four sharps and four flats:

- major
- pentatonic major
- natural minor
- pentatonic minor
- harmonic minor

- Blues scales: C, G, D, A, E, F, B♭, E♭ and A♭.
- Dorian modal scales: D, A, E, B, F#, G, C, F and B♭.
- Mixolydian modal scales: G, D, A, E, B, C, F, B♭ and E♭.

The scales that have been added for the Grade Five exam are:

- major: E and A♭
- pentatonic major: E and A♭
- natural minor: C# and F
- pentatonic minor: C# and F
- harmonic minor: C# and F
- blues scales: E and A♭
- Dorian modal scales: D, A, E, B, F#, G, C, F and B♭
- Mixolydian modal scales: G, D, A, E, B, C, F, B♭ and E♭

In this book we will only cover in detail these additional scales, so if you are unsure about any of the other requirements you should study the previous handbooks in this series.

So that the scales learnt in theory can be used effectively in a practical way, you should be able to do the following:

- Write out, or identify, each scale using standard *music notation* (adding or identifying the key signature where appropriate). You can write your answers in either the treble clef or the bass clef.
- Write out, or identify, the *scale spelling* of each scale.

the theory

major and natural minor scales

Major scales and *natural minor scales* are constructed using a combination of *whole steps* (whole tones) and *half steps* (semitones).

Major scales are constructed using the following pattern of whole steps and half steps.

W W H W W W H

Here is the E major scale as an example.

notes:	E	F#	G#	A	B	C#	D#	E
pattern:		W	W	H	W	W	W	H

Natural minor scales are constructed using the following step-pattern:

W H W W H W W

Here is the F natural minor scale as an example.

notes:	F	G	A♭	B♭	C	D♭	E♭	F
pattern:		W	H	W	W	H	W	W

pentatonic scales

Pentatonic major scales are made up of five notes taken from the major scale with the same keynote. The five notes are the 1st, 2nd, 3rd, 5th and 6th. Notice that it is the 4th and 7th notes of the major scale that are omitted to create a pentatonic major scale. The notes of the E pentatonic major scale are therefore E, F#, G#, B and C#. (When played or written as a scale the octave is also included.)

Pentatonic minor scales are made up of five notes (the 1st, 3rd, 4th, 5th and 7th) taken from the natural minor scale with the same keynote. Notice that it is the 2nd and 6th notes of the natural minor scale that are omitted to create a pentatonic minor scale. The notes of the F pentatonic minor scale are therefore F, A♭, B♭, C and E♭. (When played or written as a scale the octave is also included.)

harmonic minor scales

The harmonic minor scale contains the same notes as the natural minor scale (that starts with the same keynote) *except that* the note on the seventh degree is raised a half step in the harmonic minor scale.

The table below shows some examples contrasting the difference between natural minor and harmonic minor scales.

C# natural minor:	C# D# E F# G# A B C#
C# harmonic minor:	C# D# E F# G# A B# C#
F natural minor:	F G A♭ B♭ C D♭ E♭ F
F harmonic minor:	F G A♭ B♭ C D♭ E F

blues scales

The *blues scale* is a six-note scale. It uses notes from the major scale, but lowers some of them by a half step. The notes taken from the major scale are the 1st, 3rd, 4th, 5th and 7th, however the 3rd, 5th and 7th notes are all lowered by one half step to create the *blue notes*. The ♭3rd and ♭7th notes replace the 3rd and 7th notes of the major scale, but the ♭5th note is used *in addition to* the 5th note of the major scale. The blues scale therefore contains the 1st, ♭3rd, 4th, ♭5th, 5th and ♭7th. (When played or written as a scale the octave is also included.)

For example:

The notes of the E blues scale are:

E G A B♭ B♮ D E

The notes of the A♭ blues scale are:

A♭ C♭ D♭ E♭♭ E♭ G♭ A♭

modal scales

Modal scales are formed by taking the notes of an existing scale but starting from a note other than the original keynote.

Two types of modal scale are required for the Grade Five exam: the Dorian modal scale and the Mixolydian modal scale.

Dorian modal scales are created by using the notes of the major scale but starting from the second degree; the second note of the major scale becomes the keynote note of the Dorian modal scale.

For example, the notes of the C major scale are: C D E F G A B C. The second note in the C major scale is D, so the Dorian modal scale which is generated from the C major scale is the D Dorian modal scale. The D note becomes the keynote of the Dorian modal scale and the remaining notes in the C major scale make up the rest of the D Dorian modal scale. The notes in the D Dorian modal scale are therefore: D E F G A B C D.

The notes of the E major scale are E F# G# A B C# D# E, so the F# Dorian modal scale would be generated because F# is the second note in the E major scale. The notes in the F# Dorian modal scale would therefore be F# G# A B C# D# E F#.

Even though the major scale and the Dorian modal scale use the same notes, because they have different keynotes they do not have the same tonality. This is because the Dorian modal scale has a flattened 3rd interval from the root to the third note and a flattened 7th interval from the root to the seventh note, whereas the major scale has a major 3rd interval from the root to the third note and a major 7th interval from the root to the seventh note.

Mixolydian modal scales are created by using the notes of the major scale but starting from the fifth degree; the fifth note of the major scale becomes the keynote of the Mixolydian modal scale.

For example, the notes of the C major scale are: C D E F G A B C. The fifth note in the C major scale is G, so the Mixolydian modal scale which is generated from the C major scale is the G Mixolydian modal scale. The G note becomes the keynote of the Mixolydian modal scale and the remaining notes in the C major scale make up the rest of the G Mixolydian modal scale. The notes in the G Mixolydian modal scale are therefore: G A B C D E F G.

The notes of the E major scale are E F# G# A C# D# E, so the B Mixolydian modal scale would be generated because B is the fifth note in the E major scale. The notes in the B Mixolydian modal scale would therefore be B C# D# E F# G# A B.

Even though the major scale and the Mixolydian modal scale use the same notes, because they have different keynotes they do not have the same tonality. This is because the Mixolydian modal scale has a flattened 7th interval from the root to the seventh note, whereas the major scale has a major 7th interval from the root to the seventh note.

scale notes

Here are the names of the notes contained within the major, pentatonic major, natural minor, pentatonic minor, harmonic minor and blues scales that have been added for the Grade Five exam.

E major:	E	F#	G#	A	B	C#	D#	E
A♭ major:	A♭	B♭	C	D♭	E♭	F	G	A♭
C# natural minor:	C#	D#	E	F#	G#	A	B	C#
F natural minor:	F	G	A♭	B♭	C	D♭	E♭	F
E pentatonic major:	E	F#	G#	B	C#	E		
A♭ pentatonic major:	A♭	B♭	C	E♭	F	A♭		
C# pentatonic minor:	C#	E	F#	G#	B	C#		
F pentatonic minor:	F	A♭	B♭	C	E♭	F		
C# harmonic minor:	C#	D#	E	F#	G#	A	B#	C#
F harmonic minor:	F	G	A♭	B♭	C	D♭	E	F
E blues:	E	G	A	B♭	B♮	D	E	
A♭ blues:	A♭	C♭	D♭	E♭♭	E♭	G♭	A♭	

Here are some examples of the Dorian and Mixolydian modal scales that are required for the Grade Five exam.

D Dorian:	D	E	F	G	A	B	C	D
F# Dorian:	F#	G#	A	B	C#	D#	E	F#
B♭ Dorian:	B♭	C	D♭	E♭	F	G	A♭	B♭
G Mixolydian:	G	A	B	C	D	E	F	G
B Mixolydian:	B	C#	D#	E	F#	G#	A	B
E♭ Mixolydian:	E♭	F	G	A♭	B♭	C	D♭	E♭

If you forget the names of the notes in any of the scales you can work them out in the following ways:

- Major and natural minor scales: use the 'step-pattern' to work out the notes of the scale. WWHWWWH for major scales, WHWWHWW for natural minor scales.

- Pentatonic major and minor scales: use the 'step-pattern' to work out the notes of the appropriate major or natural minor scales and then select the five notes that you need for the pentatonic scale you require.

- Harmonic minor scales: work out the appropriate natural minor scale using the 'step-pattern' and then raise the 7th note of the scale by a half step.

- Blues scales: work out the appropriate major scale using the 'step-pattern', and then select the six notes you need for the blues scale, lowering the 3rd, 5th and 7th degrees by a half step. Remember that you need to include both the flattened 5th and the perfect 5th degrees of the scale.

- Dorian modal scales: work out which major scale the mode is created from by moving down a whole step (whole tone). Work out the notes in the major scale by using the step-pattern and then re-write the scale starting from the second note.

- Mixolydian modal scales: work out which major scale the mode is created from by moving down a perfect fifth interval. Work out the notes in the major scale by using the step-pattern and then re-write the scale starting from the fifth note.

Remember that in each of these scales (apart from on the fifth degree of the blues scale) each letter name should only be used once (except for the repetition of the keynote at the octave).

key signatures and scale notation

Each key signature represents both a major key and its relative minor key.

For example:

Four sharps – F#, C#, G# and D# – is the key signature for both E major and C# minor.

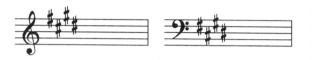

Four flats – Bb, Eb, Ab and Db – is the key signature for both Ab major and F minor.

You can usually identify whether the key of a piece of music is major or minor by its overall sound; sometimes you can also identify this by seeing which note the melody begins or ends with. If a piece of music has four flats in the key signature and begins and ends on an Ab note it is likely to be in the key of Ab major; if it begins and ends on an F note it is likely to be in the key of F minor. If the chords for a song are shown, then you can normally identify the key from the first and last chord.

writing harmonic minor scales

Harmonic minor scales are written using the appropriate minor key signature and then using an accidental to raise the note on the seventh degree of the scale by a half step.

■ If the 7th note is a natural, according to the key signature, then the accidental will need to be a sharp. For example, the key signature for C# minor means that the 7th degree is B natural: so in the scale of C# harmonic minor the 7th note will be B#.

■ If the 7th note is a flat, according to the key signature, then the accidental will need to be a natural. For example, the key signature for F minor means that the 7th note is Eb: so in the scale of F harmonic minor the 7th note will be E♮.

blues key signatures

Blues music does not fit neatly into the traditional rules of music theory that were originally developed for classical music. Because blues scales have a minor third interval between the 1st and 3rd notes of the scale, it might appear that they should use minor key signatures. However, it is generally considered that major key signatures are more appropriate for blues. The reason for this is that blues music is usually based on 'dominant harmony' – in other words, the chordal accompaniment to a blues normally consists of dominant 7th chords. As dominant 7th chords are essentially 'major' chords, this creates an underlying 'major harmony' which is best reflected by the use of major key signatures. The fact that the melody or improvisation uses *flattened* notes against these major chords is simply a reflection of the method that blues music uses to create the musical tensions which form the core of the 'blues' sound.

Although using major key signatures means that a number of accidentals will have to be used when notating music taken from the blues scale, this is actually an advantage as it immediately demonstrates to the reader that the written music is blues-based and not in a standard major or minor key.

The key signature for each blues scale is therefore the same as for the major scale with the same starting pitch. For example, the E blues scale has a key signature of four sharps – F#, C#, G# and D# and the Ab blues scale has a key signature of four flats – Bb, Eb, Ab and Db.

Remember that the above is a combination of two musical traditions and reflects the most common current usage. For blues scales and keys, the key signature only tells you what the key centre is – it does NOT tell you which notes are in the scale. In fact, each blues scale will need to use several accidentals as a result of the key signature.

writing blues

In traditional music notation it is not standard practice to notate a ♮5th and a b5th in a scale (instead a #4th is often substituted). However, in music from a blues tradition this method best reflects the derivation and common usage of the ♭5 note. For example, the E blues scale contains both a B♭ and a B♮.

E blues

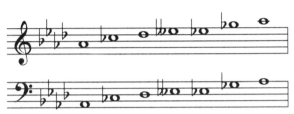

A♭ blues

> **Enharmonic spellings**
>
> The C♭ note in the A♭ blues scale is another way of describing the pitch of 'B'. Whilst there would be no difference in the sound of either version, it is important in all scales that the pitch name of the note matches its position in the scale. For example, the A♭ blues scale uses a 'double flat' (E♭♭) to notate the ♭5th because it is the fifth note (E♭) which is lowered and not the fourth note (D♭) which is raised.

modal scales

Using key signatures with modal based music is not incorrect, however, this method could be misleading as the key signature would not prepare the reader for the modal key centres. For example, to use a key signature with one sharp (F♯) for both the A Dorian modal scale and the D Mixolydian modal scale (both of which are created from the G major scale) would be very misleading to a performer. If a piece of music has one sharp in the key signature, a performer might expect the key centre to be either G major or E minor. The key signature would not prepare the performer for a key centre of A, (for music based on the A Dorian modal scale), or D (for music based on the D Mixolydian scale). Therefore, to ensure clarity of tonality, we recommend that you write modal scales, and music based on them, using accidentals rather than key signatures.

Here are some examples of the Dorian and Mixolydian modal scales.

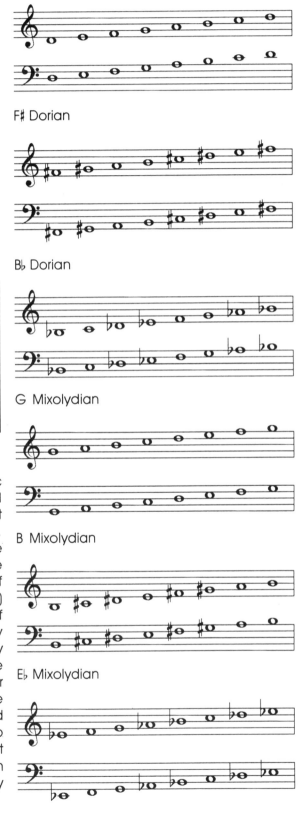

D Dorian

F♯ Dorian

B♭ Dorian

G Mixolydian

B Mixolydian

E♭ Mixolydian

scale spellings

In popular music, instead of using the letter names of the notes in a scale, musicians often use numbers. This is called the *scale spelling*. Each note of the scale is given a number, starting with the keynote as '1'.

For example, in the E major scale the notes would be numbered as follows:

E	F#	G#	A	B	C#	D#	E
1	2	3	4	5	6	7	8

The numbers refer to the *intervals* between the keynote and each other note in the scale. For example, rather than talking about the B note in the scale of E, pop musicians might refer to it as the 5th of E.

Each type of scale has a unique scale spelling. This enables easy comparison between different scale types. Below are the scale spellings for the various scales you should know at this grade.

<u>Major scales</u> are numbered like this:

1 2 3 4 5 6 7 8

All other scales are numbered in comparison to the major scale.

<u>Natural minor scales</u> are numbered like this:

1 2 ♭3 4 5 ♭6 ♭7 8

<u>Harmonic minor scales</u> are numbered like this:

1 2 ♭3 4 5 ♭6 7 8

There follows a brief explanation as to why the natural minor and harmonic minor scales are numbered this way. However, in the exam you will only be asked to identify, or write out, the scale spellings.

Supplementary explanation

The appearance of a ♭ sign in a scale spelling does not mean that the note which occurs on that scale degree is necessarily a flat note. Instead, the flat sign is used, in this instance, as a method of indicating that this scale degree forms a *smaller* interval (usually a minor, but sometimes a diminished interval) when compared to the major scale – i.e. the distance between the keynote and this scale degree is a half step smaller than the distance between the keynote and the corresponding scale degree in the major scale with the same keynote. For example, the interval between E to G (the third degree of the E natural minor scale) is a half step smaller than the interval between E and G# (the third degree of the E major scale). In fact, the 3rd, 6th and 7th degrees of the natural minor scale are all 'minor' intervals when compared to major scale. (You can work this out for yourself by counting the number of half steps between the keynotes and these degrees of the scales). In the harmonic minor scale, only the 3rd and 6th degrees are 'flattened' in comparison with the major scale. Although the meaning is exactly the same, pop musicians generally prefer to call these smaller intervals 'flattened' (rather than minor), and consequently a ♭ is placed before them to indicate this. An example is given below, showing the comparison between scale types and the consequent difference in the scale spelling.

E major scale

E	F#	G#	A	B	C#	D#	E
1	2	3	4	5	6	7	8

E natural minor scale

E	F#	G	A	B	C	D	E
1	2	♭3	4	5	♭6	♭7	8

E harmonic minor scale

E	F#	G	A	B	C	D#	E
1	2	♭3	4	5	♭6	7	8

<u>Pentatonic major scales</u> are numbered like this:

1 2 3 5 6 8

The scale spelling of the pentatonic major scale is based on that of the major scale, but because the pentatonic major scale doesn't include the 4th or 7th notes of the major scale, these scale numbers are omitted.

<u>Pentatonic minor scales</u> are numbered like this:

$$1 \flat3\ 4\ 5\ \flat7\ 8$$

The scale spelling of the pentatonic minor scale is based on the natural minor scale, but because the pentatonic minor scale doesn't include the 2nd or ♭6th notes of the natural minor scale, these scale numbers are omitted.

<u>Blues scales</u> are numbered like this:

$$1 \flat3\ 4\ \flat5\ 5\ \flat7\ 8$$

There follows a brief explanation as to why the blues scale is numbered this way. In the exam, however, you will only be asked to identify, or write out, the scale spelling.

Supplementary explanation

The scale spelling of the blues scale is numbered in comparison to the major scale with the same starting note. The blues scale contains the 4th and 5th notes of the major scale, but not the 2nd or 6th notes. In the blues scale, the 3rd and 7th degrees are *flattened* (or *minor*) intervals because the intervals between the keynote and these scale degrees are all a half step smaller than the intervals between the keynote and the corresponding scale degrees in the major scale. The additional note – the ♭5th – creates a *flattened* (or *diminished*) interval. This is because this interval is one half step smaller than the interval created by the ♮5th note which is also contained in the scale. The full name for the interval between the 1st and 5th degrees in all the scales covered so far (including the blues scale) is a *perfect fifth*. Unlike the other intervals we have looked at, when *perfect 5th* intervals are made smaller by one half step they are not called 'minor' 5th intervals, instead they are known as *flattened* or *diminished 5th* intervals.

<u>Dorian modal scales</u> are numbered like this:

$$1\ 2 \flat3\ 4\ 5\ 6\ \flat7\ 8$$

<u>Mixolydian modal scales</u> are numbered like this:

$$1\ 2\ 3\ 4\ 5\ 6\ \flat7\ 8$$

The Dorian and Mixolydian modal scales are numbered with flat signs in front of some of the numbers for the same reason that the natural minor and harmonic minor scales are also numbered like this: i.e. the intervals from the keynote note to each of these scale degrees are all one half step smaller than the corresponding intervals in the major scale.

comparing scales

You can use your knowledge of major scales and scale spellings to work out the notes contained in all other scales.

major scale:	1	2	3	4	5	6	7	8
G major:	G	A	B	C	D	E	F♯	G
pentatonic major:	1	2	3		5	6		8
G pentatonic major:	G	A	B		D	E		G
natural minor:	1	2	♭3	4	5	♭6	♭7	8
G natural minor:	G	A	B♭	C	D	E♭	F	G
pentatonic minor:	1	♭3	4		5	♭7		8
G pentatonic minor:	G	B♭	C		D	F		G
harmonic minor:	1	2	♭3	4	5	♭6	7	8
G harmonic minor:	G	A	B♭	C	D	E♭	F♯	G
blues:	1	♭3	4	♭5	5	♭7		8
G blues:	G	B♭	C	D♭	D♮	F		G
Dorian modal scale:	1	2	♭3	4	5	6	♭7	8
G Dorian modal scale:	G	A	B♭	C	D	E	F	G
Mixolydian modal scale:	1	2	3	4	5	6	♭7	8
G Mixolydian modal scale:	G	A	B	C	D	E	F	G

Alternatively, scales can also be compared directly with each other (without reference to the major scale). For example:

■ the pentatonic minor scale is the same as the natural minor scale with the 2nd and 6th notes omitted;

■ the harmonic minor scale is the same as the natural minor but with the 7th note raised a half step;

■ the blues scale, except for the addition of the ♭5th note, is exactly the same as the pentatonic minor scale;

■ the Dorian modal scale is the same as the natural minor scale, except for the interval between the keynote and the 6th note – which is flattened in the natural minor scale;

■ the Mixolydian modal scale is the same as the major scale, except for the interval between the keynote and the 7th note – which is flattened in the Mixolydian modal scale.

Below are some examples of the types of questions that candidates may be asked in this section of the exam. If you can't answer a question, then carefully re-read the preceding chapter and, if necessary, refer to the earlier books in this series.

When answering questions that involve writing scales in notation, you can write them in either the treble or bass clef. Either way, you need only write them ascending using whole notes.

Q1. Write one octave of the D Mixolydian modal scale, without using a key signature, in either the treble or bass clef.

A1.

Q2. Using the correct key signature and appropriate accidentals, write one octave of the E blues scale in either the treble or bass clef.

A2.

Q3. Using the correct key signature, write one octave of the harmonic minor scale that has four flats in the key signature. Use either the treble or bass clef.

A3.

Q4. Which scale has the following scale spelling: 1 2 ♭3 4 5 ♭6 7 8 ?

A4. _____

Q5. Write out the scale spelling of the Dorian modal scale.

A5. _____

Section Two – chords

In this section of the exam, you should have a good knowledge of the chords set for previous grades but extended to a range of keys to 4 sharps and 4 flats:

- Triads: major, minor, diminished, sus 2, sus 4 and 5th 'power chords'.
- Major 7th, minor 7th, dominant 7th and minor 7th ♭5 chords.

In addition, you may be asked to write out and identify any of the chord types listed below built from major and natural minor scales within a range of keys to 4 sharps and 4 flats:

- Major 6th and minor 6th chords.
- 1st and 2nd inversions of major and minor triads.

plus:

- Dominant 7th chords from harmonic minor scales to a range of 4 sharps and 4 flats.
- Diminished 7th chords.

So that the chords learnt in theory can be used effectively in a practical way, you should be able to do the following:

- Use chord symbols to identify the chords.
- Write out, and identify, each chord using standard music notation. You can write your answers in either the treble clef or the bass clef.
- Write out, and identify, the chord spelling of each chord, and name the intervals between the root and each chord tone.

the theory

chord construction

The chord types that have been added at this grade are explained below. The construction of all the other required triads and seventh chords has been fully covered in the preceding books in this series.

6th chords

The major 6th chord is a major triad with the 6th note of the major scale added. For example, C major 6th contains the notes: C E G A.

The minor 6th chord is a minor triad with the 6th note of the major scale (with the same starting note) added. For example, C minor 6th contains the notes: C E♭ G A.

Notice that in both major 6th and minor 6th chords, the '6th' refers to a major 6th interval from the root. The 'major' and 'minor' in the two chord names refer to the type of triad, not to the 6th interval.

inversions of major and minor triads

In previous grades all the chords have been written in *root position*. This means that each chord is written starting with the lowest note, then the third, then fifth and then, where appropriate, the sixth or seventh.

Chord inversions involve changing the order of notes within a chord. Strictly speaking, this involves 'inverting' the lowest note of the chord to become the highest, whilst maintaining the progressive order of the other notes. However, in popular music the term 'inversion' is widely used (particularly amongst guitarists) simply to refer to any chord in which a chord tone other than the root is placed as the lowest note in the chord.

There are two inversions that you are required to know for the Grade Five exam. You are only required to apply these inversions to major and minor triads:

- 1st inversion is where the root note is displaced (usually, but not necessarily, to the top of the chord) and the third becomes the lowest note.

- 2nd inversion is where the root note is displaced (usually, but not necessarily, to the middle of the chord) and the fifth becomes the lowest note.

<u>dominant 7th chords from the harmonic minor</u>

The chord that is built, by taking four alternate notes, starting on the fith degree of the natural minor scale is always a minor 7th. However, the chord that is built on the fifth degree of the *harmonic* minor scale is always a *dominant 7th*.

For example:

B harmonic minor	F#7
B C# D E F# G A# B	F# A# C# E
F# harmonic minor	C#7
F# G# A B C# D E# F#	C# E# G# B
C# harmonic minor	G#7
C# D# E F# G# A B# C#	G# B# D# F#

<u>diminished 7th chords</u>

Diminished 7ths chords are unusual because every interval between each chord tone is equivalent to a minor third. This means that the diminished 7th chord is made up of a root, a flat 3rd, a flat 5th and a double flat 7th. For example:

- the notes in the C diminished 7th chord are C E♭ G♭ B♭♭. B♭♭ is the same pitch as A, however it is called B♭♭ in this instance because it is based on the 7th degree of the scale – rather than the 6th.

- the notes in the E diminished 7th chord are E G B♭ D♭.

- the notes in the A♭ diminished 7th chord are A♭ C♭ E♭♭ G♭♭. E♭♭ is the same pitch as D, but in this instance it is called E♭♭ because it is the flattened (diminished) 5th note (not the sharpened 4th).

chord symbols

Here are the chord symbols for the additional chord types set for Grade Five – written using C as the root of each chord. The chord symbols shown in the middle column are those most commonly used (and those recommended for use in the exam). A range of alternative symbols are sometimes used by pop musicians – these are shown in the right hand column.

Major sixth	C6	Cma6 CM6
Minor sixth	Cm6	Cmi6 Cmin6 C-6
Diminished seventh	C°7	Cdim7
Major 1st inversion	C/E	C
Major 2nd inversion	C/G	C
Minor 1st inversion	Cm/E♭	Cm
Minor 2nd inversion	Cm/G	Cm

Note that inversions are not always written out in chord symbols; in popular music the inversion to be used (if any) is often left to the discretion of the performer.

chord notation

Here are examples of the additional chords required for Grade Five, written out in the treble clef and the bass clef. To work out the notes contained in any of the other chords required for Grade Five, you should either refer to the 'chord spelling' section (later on in this chapter) or study the preceding books in this series.

Emaj7

D♭maj7

G#m7

B♭m7

B7

F♯7

C♯7

G♯7

E♭7

D♯m7♭5

Gm7♭5

C6

A♭6

E6

Am6

Fm6

C♯m6

C°7

E°7

A♭°7

Here are the C major and C minor triads in root position, 1st inversion and 2nd inversion.

chord spellings

Pop musicians often use numbers to talk about the notes in a chord. This is called the *chord spelling*. Each note in the chord is given a number, which refers to the *interval* between that note and the root of the chord. Each type of chord has a unique chord spelling and all chord types are numbered, and the intervals named, in comparison to the major 7th chord (or major scale). This enables easy comparison between different chord types.

The table below gives the chord spelling of the chord types required for the Grade Five exam.

Major triads	1	3	5	
Minor triads	1	♭3	5	
Diminished triads	1	♭3	♭5	
Sus 2	1	2	5	
Sus 4	1	4	5	
5th 'power chords'	1	5	8	
Major 7th chords	1	3	5	7
Minor 7th chords	1	♭3	5	♭7
Dominant 7th chords	1	3	5	♭7
Minor 7th♭5 chords	1	♭3	♭5	♭7
Major 6th chords	1	3	5	6
Minor 6th chords	1	♭3	5	6
Diminished 7th chords	1	♭3	♭5	♭♭7
Major triads 1st inversion	3	5	1	
Minor triads 1st inversion	♭3	5	1	
Major triads 2nd inversion	5	1	3	
Minor triads 2nd inversion	5	1	♭3	

Some chords contain a ♭ before the number in the chord spelling, to indicate that the interval is one half step smaller than the corresponding interval in a major chord or scale. For example, between E and G♯ (root and 3rd in Emaj7) there are four half steps, whilst between E and G (root and 3rd in Em7) there are only three half steps. Consequently, the third in a minor 7th chord is called a flattened 3rd (♭3) or minor 3rd interval.

For similar reasons, the seventh in a minor 7th, minor 7th ♭5 and dominant 7th chord is a called a flattened 7th (♭7) or minor 7th interval, and the fifth in a minor 7th ♭5 and diminished 7th chord is known as a flattened 5th (♭5) or diminished 5th interval. The ♭♭ sign is used in the diminished 7th chord as this interval is a whole tone (i.e. two half steps) smaller than a major seventh interval.

comparing chords

Chords can also be compared to each other, without reference to the major scale. For example:

■ a major 6th chord differs from a minor 6th chord in that it has a major 3rd, rather than a minor 3rd, interval from the root.

■ a diminished 7th chord only differs from a minor 7th ♭5 chord, in that it has a double flattened 7th, rather than a flattened 7th, interval from the root.

■ a major triad 1st inversion contains the same notes as a standard (root position) major triad, the only difference is that in 1st inversion the 3rd of the chord is written and played as the lowest note of the chord.

■ a minor triad 1st inversion contains the same notes as a standard (root position) minor triad, however in 1st inversion the 3rd of the chord is written and played as the lowest note of the chord.

■ a major triad 2nd inversion contains the same notes as a standard (root position) major triad, however in 2nd inversion the 5th of the chord is written and played as the lowest note of the chord.

■ a minor triad 2nd inversion contains the same notes as a standard (root position) minor triad, however in 2nd inversion the 5th of the chord is written and played as the lowest note of the chord.

Below are some examples of types of questions that candidates may be asked in this section of the exam. If you can't answer a question, then carefully re-read the preceding chapter and, if necessary, refer to the earlier books in this series.

When answering questions that involve writing chords in notation, you can write your answers in either the treble clef or the bass clef. The notes of each chord should be written in *root position* unless stated otherwise.

Q1.   Write out E6 using standard notation in either the treble or bass clef.

A1.

Q2.   Name the following root position chord.

A2.   _____

Q3.   Write out the chord spelling of the minor 6th chord.

A3.   _____

Q4.   What type of interval is there between the root and the seventh in a minor 7th ♭5 chord?

A4.   _____

Q5.   Write out F#m in 2nd inversion, in either the treble or bass clef.

A5.

Section Three – rhythm notation

In this section of the exam you will be asked to use some of the following note and rest values in $\frac{2}{4}$ $\frac{3}{4}$ $\frac{4}{4}$ $\frac{6}{8}$ $\frac{9}{8}$ or $\frac{12}{8}$ time:

- whole notes (semibreves)
- half notes (minims)
- quarter notes (crotchets)
- eighth notes (quavers)
- sixteenth notes (semiquavers)

- whole rests (semibreve rests)
- half rests (minim rests)
- quarter rests (crotchet rests)
- eighth rests (quaver rests)
- sixteenth rests (semiquaver rests)

- dotted notes and dotted rests (for all of the above, where appropriate, except for sixteenth notes)
- tied notes
- triplets

So that the rhythm notation learnt in theory can be used effectively in a practical way, you should be able to do the following:

- Group notes and rests correctly.
- Compose rhythmic patterns using the note and rest values listed.

the theory

If you require information on the fundamentals of rhythm notation, including the use of tied notes, you should study the earlier books in this series.

triplets

Triplets are used where a note is divided into three instead of two:

- In the time of a whole note, three half notes are played instead of two.
- In the time of a half note, three quarter notes are played instead of two.
- In the time of a quarter note, three eighth notes are played instead of two.
- In the time of an eighth note, three sixteenth notes are played instead of two.

Once a triplet has been indicated, any equivalent combination of notes can be played. This means that:

- three half note triplets (or their equivalent) last for 1 whole note
- three quarter note triplets (or their equivalent) last for 1 half note

- three eighth note triplets (or their equivalent) last for 1 quarter note
- three sixteenth note triplets (or their equivalent) last for 1 eighth note

Triplets are usually indicated by a bracket with a '3'. However, you may sometimes see them written with just the '3' – particularly in the case of beamed notes.

time signatures

$\frac{2}{4}$ $\frac{3}{4}$ and $\frac{4}{4}$ are all known as *simple time signatures*. In these time signatures each beat is represented by a quarter note and can be divided into two.

$\frac{6}{8}$ $\frac{9}{8}$ and $\frac{12}{8}$ are *compound time signatures*. Although in $\frac{12}{8}$ time there is an equivalent of twelve eighth notes in a bar, there are only four main beats: four dotted quarter notes – each comprising three eighth note pulses. So in $\frac{12}{8}$ time, each of its four beats can be divided into three:

In $\frac{9}{8}$ time there are three dotted quarter note beats, whilst there are two in $\frac{6}{8}$ time.

grouping of notes and rests

There are certain rules about how notes and rests can be grouped. These rules exist in music notation so that all the beats of the bar can be clearly identified, and consequently the written music is easier to read.

At this level you should be aware of the following rules and the exceptions to these rules.

simple time signatures

RULE 1

Quarter notes, and notes shorter than a quarter note, are beamed together when they belong to one beat.

For example:

Exceptions

i) In a bar of $\frac{4}{4}$ time, you can beam together all eighth notes that are in the first half of a bar (beats one and two) or in the second half of the bar (beats three and four). However, you should not beam together notes across the middle of the bar (beats two and three).

ii) In $\frac{2}{4}$ and $\frac{3}{4}$ time you can beam together all eighth notes within a bar.

For example:

RULE 2

When you write rests, each beat and each half beat must be completed with the appropriate rests. This is because it is much easier to read music if you can clearly see where each beat and each half beat starts.

For example:

Exceptions

i) In a bar of $\frac{4}{4}$ time you can write a half (minim) rest in the first half of the bar (beats one and two) or in the second half of the bar (beats three and four). However, you should not write a half rest in the middle of the bar (beats two and three) – instead you should use two quarter (crotchet) rests.

ii) The whole note (semibreve) rest (also known as the 'whole bar' rest) indicates a whole bar rest in all popular time signatures, including $\frac{2}{4}$ and $\frac{3}{4}$. Consequently, dotted half note rests are not used in $\frac{3}{4}$; a whole bar rest is used instead.

iii) Although it is normally easier to see all the main beats if you write rests out in full (with each beat having a rest of its own where needed), you can use dotted rests in certain places (such as at the start of the bar in $\frac{4}{4}$ time).

For example:

compound time signatures

RULE 1

Notes shorter than a dotted quarter note should be grouped together when they belong to one beat. This helps to clarify where the underlying dotted quarter note beat is.

For example, in $\frac{12}{8}$ time the first three eighth note pulses (including any combination of eighth notes and sixteenth notes) should be beamed together. Similarly, each successive group of three eighth note pulses should be beamed together.

This is correct

The following bar is *incorrect* because, although it contains the same order of notes as the example above, the notes are grouped incorrectly.

RULE 2

The same rule for writing rests in simple time – that each beat must be completed with the appropriate rests – applies in compound time. When you write rests in compound time you must remember that each beat is equivalent to a dotted quarter note.

This is correct.

This is *incorrect* because it is written as though in $\frac{3}{4}$ time.

Exception

The whole note (semibreve) rest indicates a whole bar rest in all popular time signatures, including compound time signatures.

There are specific additional rules about how the rests within each beat can be written. Remember, a beat in compound time lasts for a dotted quarter note.

- If the first two eighth note pulses of a beat are silent, a single quarter note rest should be used.

- If the last two eighth note pulses of a beat are silent, then two eighth note rests (rather than a single quarter note rest) should be used.

This is correct

This is *incorrect*

Rests within triplets

When you write rests as part of a triplet, you should follow the same rules that apply to compound time signatures. If the first two pulses of a set of eighth note triplets are meant to be silent then a single quarter note rest should be used. However, if the last two pulses of a set of eighth note triplets are meant to be silent, then two eighth note rests (rather than a single quarter note rest) should be used. This principle applies to all types of triplets, not just eighth note triplets.

This is correct

This is *incorrect*

Below are some examples of the types of questions that candidates may be asked in this section of the exam. If you can't answer a question, then carefully re-read the preceding chapter and, if necessary, refer to the earlier books in this series.

Q1. Re-write the following bar correctly.

A1.

Q2. Using a clef and pitch of your choice, write a four bar rhythm in $\frac{4}{4}$ time. Use any combination of notes and rests, but include some quarter note (crotchet) triplets, eighth note (quaver) triplets and at least one tie.

A2.

Q3. Using a clef and pitch of your choice, write a two bar rhythm in $\frac{12}{8}$ time. Use at least one tie and any combination of: dotted quarter notes (dotted crotchets), eighth notes (quavers), sixteenth notes and some of the equivalent rests.

A3.

Section Four – popular music

There are three areas of popular music that candidates will be asked questions on in this section of the exam:

- influential groups, vocalists and instrumentalists
- commonly used instruments
- commonly used performance directions

influential musicians

At this grade you are expected to have a broad knowledge of influential popular music groups, vocalists and instrumentalists from 1950 onwards, together with an awareness of how their music was influenced by musicians of earlier periods.

In the exam you will be asked to write a brief essay, of approximately 200 to 300 words, describing the musical career of ONE musician or group *of your choice* (from a given list).

In the exam *only one* of the lists of groups and musicians shown below will be given. You will NOT be told before the exam which list will be set. Therefore, to ensure that you are prepared for this section of the exam, it is essential that you research one group or musician from all four lists. (www.BooksForMusic.com features a range of suitable reference books.)

In your essay you should include some information about:

a) the development of their musical career, including significant dates

b) group members and the instruments played, or the groups/musicians the musician has played with

c) recordings, including hit singles and albums

The main focus of the essay should be on:

d) the main features of their music

e) an explanation of how their music was influenced by musicians from earlier periods

Here are the four lists of groups and musicians:

List A	List B	List C	List D
The Beatles	Elvis Presley	The Rolling Stones	Jimi Hendrix
Chuck Berry	Led Zepplin	Madonna	David Bowie
Bob Dylan	Michael Jackson	James Brown	Nirvana
Eric Clapton	The Sex Pistols	Bob Marley	Pink Floyd
The Who	Little Richard	Abba	Spice Girls
Diana Ross	Oasis	Buddy Holly	Metallica
The Doors	Sting	Van Halen	Garth Brooks
The Grateful Dead	Tina Turner	Aretha Franklin	Queen
Stevie Wonder	The Beach Boys	Kraftwerk	Grandmaster Flash
The Eagles	Otis Redding	Bruce Springsteen	Black Sabbath

So that you have a good knowledge of the instruments that are commonly used in popular music, you may be asked questions about the following instruments:

- electric and acoustic guitars
- bass guitars
- keyboards
- drum kit and percussion
- saxophones
- brass instruments

Below is a description of each of the instruments – giving all the information you need to know about each instrument for the Grade Five exam. We recommend that you try to hear each of the instruments being played – either live, or at least, on a recording.

electric and acoustic guitars

notes are written one octave higher than their actual pitch (using the treble clef). The diagrams below show the range of notes that can comfortably be played on most models of guitar:

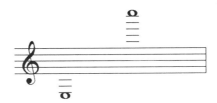

The normal range of a standard acoustic guitar is:

notation and range

The six strings on a guitar are normally tuned to E, A, D, G, B and E, starting from the lowest string. There are two octaves between the two E strings. Different notes are produced through changing the length of a string by the player pressing on different places on the fingerboard of the guitar. The fingerboard is divided into half steps (semitones) by the use of metal frets.

The highest note that can be played on a guitar can vary depending upon the model of the instrument being used. To avoid leger lines and so make music easier for guitarists to read,

Music for guitarists can also written be in tablature (TAB). This is a system that uses six lines to represent the six strings of the guitar. A number written on the string indicates which fret is to be played. A zero indicates that the string is played open.

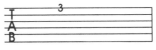

This example means play on the third fret of the high E string.

Guitarists often .improvise rhythm and lead parts from chord symbols, rather than read notation.

sound production

Although the strings can be picked with the fingers, normally in popular music a small plastic device known as a *plectrum* (or *pick*) is used to strike the strings – which can be played simultaneously to create chords or individually for single-note lead playing.

On electric guitars (which normally have solid, or semi-solid, wooden bodies) the sound is produced by the vibration of the steel strings being electrically 'picked up' by an in-built device called a *pick up* and then amplified. On acoustic guitars the sound is also produced by the vibration of the strings, but with just the hollow body of the guitar amplifying the sound.

An electric guitar needs to be played through an *amplifier* and *speaker* in order to be heard. The term *amp* can refer to an amplifier and speaker contained in one unit, or a unit which contains only an amplifier. In the latter case, a separate unit containing a speaker is needed. This is often referred to as a *cab* (short for speaker cabinet). The distinctive sound of an electric guitar is created by the interaction of the guitar, amplifier and speaker. In addition, various electronic effects can be wired-in to create a wide range of different sounds. Some standard guitar effects are

a) distortion/overdrive

b) reverb and echo/delay

c) chorus

d) wah-wah

e) phaser

Although acoustic guitars can be played without amplification, they usually require it during performances in order to match the volume of other instruments. Acoustic guitars can be amplified by placing a microphone in front of the 'sound-hole' of the guitar, or by attaching a *pick-up*.

function

A guitarist has two main functions in popular music:

1) To play *rhythm guitar*. Rhythm guitar parts often consist of chords played in repeated rhythmic patterns which link with the bass and drum parts. In this context the guitarist can be seen as part of 'the rhythm section'.

2) To play *lead guitar*. In this context the guitar is a *lead* or *soloing* instrument. Lead guitar parts are sometimes pre-prepared riffs or melodies, but solos are often *improvised*. The majority of lead guitar involves single note playing, although it can also incorporate *double stops* or chords.

bass guitars

notation and range

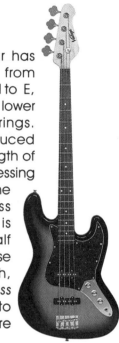

The standard bass guitar has four strings that, starting from the lowest string, are tuned to E, A, D and G – an octave lower than standard guitar strings. Different notes are produced through changing the length of a string by the player pressing on different places on the fingerboard of the bass guitar. The fingerboard is normally divided into half steps (semitones), by the use of metal frets, although, some players use *fretless* basses to enable them to *slide* between notes more easily.

The highest note that can be played on a bass guitar can vary by a whole step or more, depending upon the model of the instrument being used. To avoid leger lines and so make music easier for bass guitarists to read, notes are written one octave higher than their actual pitch (using the bass clef). The diagram below shows the range of written notes that can comfortably be played on most models of bass guitar:

In recent years, five string basses (which have an extra B string added below the E string) have become increasingly used in some forms of popular music. Occasionally, six string basses (where in addition to the B string, a C string is added above the G string) are also used by some players.

Bass players often improvise bass lines from chord symbols, but music for the bass can be notated in the bass clef and also sometimes in bass tablature. This is similar to the guitar tablature explained above, but with a reduced number of tablature lines to reflect the number of bass strings.

<u>sound production</u>

Bass strings are normally picked with the fingers, although some players prefer to use a *plectrum*.

Although some chords can be played on the bass guitar, most bass parts are single-note lines.

The sound of a bass guitar is produced by the vibration of the steel strings being electrically 'picked up' by the instrument's in-built *pick up* and then amplified. Bass amplifiers and speakers have different specifications to guitar amplifiers, as they are built to reproduce the lower frequency range of the bass guitar.

Electronic effects units (such as compression, chorus, octaver and phaser) can be connected between the bass guitar and the amplifier, but usually bass guitars are played without effects.

<u>function</u>

The fundamental role of the bass player is to be the link between the rhythm stated by the drums and the harmony stated by the guitar or keyboard.

keyboards

Although pianos are the most traditional of all modern keyboard instruments, in contemporary popular music electric pianos, electronic keyboards and synthesisers are more commonly used. Collectively, these are known as *keyboards*.

<u>notation and range</u>

Keyboards are made in many different sizes, but the notes are always laid out like a piano – with the white keys producing the natural notes (C D E F G A B) and the black keys producing the flats and sharps.

The range of a keyboard will vary depending on the model, but it is common for the keys themselves to cover at least five octaves, with the C below the treble clef being in the middle. Keyboards often have a *transpose* function which means that the range can be increased by assigning different pitches to the keys.

Standard notation for keyboard instruments uses two staffs (staves), one in the treble clef and one in the bass clef.

In popular music, keyboard players often improvise from chord symbols rather than read notation.

<u>sound production</u>

The keys on pianos and on good quality keyboards are normally *touch sensitive*. This means that the keys respond to how hard or softly the player touches them and enables the player to play with greater expression. Some keyboards also have *weighted* keys, to re-create the feel of a piano.

Pianos have foot pedals attached that enable the player to either strengthen and sustain notes, or to soften and mute notes. Some keyboards also have similar pedals, particularly a sustain or volume pedal.

Electronic keyboards usually have a variety of in-built piano and organ sounds, as well as a wide range of other *instrumental* sounds which re-create the sound of specific instruments. *Sampled* sounds (where real instruments have been digitally recorded) are usually more realistic than *synthesised* sounds, which are created electronically. Keyboards can also have many unique *synthesised* sounds, which do not emulate the sound of traditional instruments, but can be interesting musical sounds in their own right.

The keys on many keyboards can be split into different sections and assigned to different sounds to allow the player to play, for example, a bass part and chords, or string and brass sounds.

Many electronic keyboards have small in-built amplifiers and speakers, but for live performances they need to be amplified to achieve sufficient volume.

function

Keyboard players can fulfil several roles:

1) To be part of the rhythm section: adding to the rhythms created by the bass, drums and guitar – as well as stating the harmony by playing chords. They might also play an additional bass part.

2) To play lead lines; both composed melodies and improvised solos.

3) (On electric keyboards). To play brass or string parts.

4) (On electric keyboards). To add texture by using *synth pads* (synthesised sounds which are used to fill out the sound – often in place of a string section).

drum kit and percussion

Drums are usually played using wooden *drumsticks* (which sometimes have nylon tips). To achieve a different and quieter sound sometimes special *brushes* are used instead of sticks.

The larger the size of the drum, the lower the pitch of the drum will be. The bass (or kick) drum is therefore the lowest pitched drum in a conventional kit.

The pitch of a drum can be changed by *tuning* it. This is achieved by increasing or decreasing the skin tension using a *drum key*. The tighter the skin is stretched the higher the pitch will be. Drums are sometimes muted with taping or mufflers to reduce any unwanted overtones.

The cymbals which complete the kit are made of metal – usually brass.

A standard drum kit is made up of the following:

a) a *bass* (or *kick*) *drum* which is struck with a foot operated pedal

b) a *snare drum*

c) one or more high *tom toms* and a low (*floor*) *tom tom*

d) a *ride cymbal* and normally one or more *crash cymbals*

e) a pair of cymbals known as a *hi hat* (which can be closed or opened with a foot operated pedal).

Drummers often play other percussion instruments apart from those included in a drum kit. There are many different percussion instruments that come from a wide variety of musical cultures. Here are some of those most commonly used in popular music:

a) Congas: usually comprising a set of at least two, and played by striking with the hands.

b) Bongos: usually played by striking with the hands.

c) Tambourine: played by shaking, or striking with the hands, causing the small cymbals to sound.

d) Triangle: played by striking with a metal beater.

e) Shakers: played by moving the 'beans' against the walls of the casing.

f) Wood block: played by striking with a wooden beater.

g) Guiro: played by scraping the ridged surface of the casing with a stick.

h) Cowbell: played by striking the metal body with a wooden beater.

i) Cabassa: played by moving the metal chain against the body of the cabassa.

notation

In popular music, drummers normally make up their own drum patterns and improvise fills. However, a basic knowledge of drum notation can be a useful way of communicating musical ideas.

Drum parts can be written in *drum notation*, where the lines and spaces on the staff are used to represent different drums and cymbals. There are some variations in how drum notation is written and sometimes a special *drum key* is shown to the left of the staff to indicate which lines represent which drum. The most common method of drum notation is shown below:

- Notes in the bottom space represent the bass drum;

- Notes in the second space up represent the floor tom;

- Notes in the third space up represent the snare drum;

- Notes in the fourth space up represent the small tom tom (usually 12")

- Notes on the fourth line up represent the 2nd tom tom (usually 13")

- The hi hat and cymbal are written as stemmed Xs above the staff. Special signs are used to indicate which is required and whether the hi hat should be played open or closed.

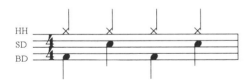

This example means the bass drum sounds on beats 1 and 3, the snare on beats 2 and 4, whilst the hi hat sounds on all 4 beats.

function

The drummer is the foundation of the rhythm section. The drum pattern is used to establish the rhythmic style of the music and also to keep time. Drum accents and fills are used to emphasise certain points of the music.

saxophone

There are several different sizes of saxophone. The two most commonly used in popular music are the *tenor saxophone* and the *alto saxophone*. *Baritone saxophones* are sometimes used as part of a *horn section* and *soprano saxophones* are sometimes used for lead solos.

range

Saxophones have a range of about two and a half octaves (without using harmonics, where notes are produced using 'fake' fingerings). The range of each saxophone is as follows:

Soprano saxophone:

Alto saxophone:

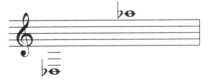

Tenor saxophone:

Baritone saxophone:

transposition and notation

Saxophones are *transposing* instruments. This is so that all four saxophones have the same fingering. Soprano and tenor saxophones are B♭ instruments, whilst alto and baritone saxophones are E♭ instruments. This means that the fingering for a C note on a soprano or tenor saxophone produces a pitch of B♭, whilst the fingering for a C note on an alto or baritone saxophone produces the pitch of E♭. When writing out music for saxophonists use the treble clef.

In order that the notes sounded are equivalent to those of non-transposing instruments, e.g. a piano, standard (concert) notation for saxophones must be transposed as follows:

- Soprano saxophone: up a whole step.

- Alto saxophone: up a major 6th.

- Tenor saxophone: up an octave and a whole step.

- Baritone saxophone: up an octave and a major 6th.

Saxophonists often improvise solos by following the chord symbols, and so solos are rarely notated.

sound production

The body of the saxophone is hollow and made of brass. Air is blown through the body via the mouthpiece, where a *reed* (a small strip of cane) is attached. The reed vibrates producing sound waves that then resonate through the body of the saxophone. Different notes are produced by pressing and releasing *pads* that cover the tone holes: this changes the body length that the sound waves resonate through.

The mouthpieces are made out of either ebonite (rubber) or metal, both of which have a different sound quality.

In a concert setting, saxophones are usually amplified by using a microphone connected to a P.A. system.

function

In popular music saxophonists have two main roles:

1) as part of a 'horn section', playing backing riffs. A typical pop music horn section would consist of a trumpet, a tenor or alto saxophone and a trombone (although sometimes baritone saxophones are used instead of trombones).

2) as a solo instrument, playing both composed melodies and improvised solos.

brass instruments

The most commonly used brass instruments in popular music are trumpets and trombones.

range

There are different types of trumpets, but the most commonly used ones are *B♭ trumpets* – which are *transposing* instruments.

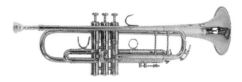

Their normal range is shown below:

Some trumpeters can play higher than this – to around the F above the treble clef stave.

There are different sizes of trombone but the most commonly used ones are the tenor trombone and the bass trombone.

The tenor trombone is higher in pitch, and is more often used in popular music, than the bass trombone.

The range of the tenor trombone is shown below:

A lead trombone player would be expected to play up to the C or D immediately above this and some trombonists can play as high as the F above that (i.e. the F on the top line of the treble clef).

Bass trombone players can reach the note of C *below* the bass clef.

Bass and tenor trombones can also play these pedal notes:

notation and transposition

Notation for B♭ trumpets is written in the treble clef, but it must be transposed up a whole step in order for it to be equivalent to standard (concert) pitch.

Both tenor and bass trombones are non-transposing instruments and in popular music trombone parts are written using the bass clef.

sound production

The sound is produced in both instruments by air being blown through the instrument: the player's lips vibrate and create sound waves which are amplified by the body of the instrument. Different notes are produced by changing the amount of tension in the lips.

Trumpets also have *valves*, each of which, when pressed, change the length of the tube and produce further notes.

In trombones the length of the tube is changed, and further notes produced, by the use of a *slide*. There are also, lesser used, *valve trombones*, which operate in a similar way to trumpets.

Trumpets and trombones use *mutes* to change the sound of the instrument. These are devices which are made out of metal, rubber or plastic and are held over the end of the instrument (where the sound comes out) so muting the volume. Some of the different mutes used are:

a) cup

b) straight

c) Harman

d) plunger

e) bucket

In a concert setting, brass instruments are sometimes amplified using microphones and a P.A. system.

function

In popular music brass players have two main roles:

1) as part of a horn section, playing backing riffs. A typical pop music horn section would consist of a trumpet, a trombone and a tenor or alto saxophone.

2) as a solo instrument, playing both composed melodies and improvised solos.

So that you have a broad knowledge of the musical signs and terminology used in popular music you will be asked questions on the following areas:

- tempo
- dynamics
- articulation
- directions for rests and repeats

So that the signs and terminology learnt in theory can be effectively used in a practical way, you should be able to:

- understand the practical differences in tempo between different bpm (metronome) markings
- explain in practical terms what different dynamic markings mean
- add dynamic markings to a chord progression or melody
- add articulation markings to a chord progression or melody
- understand and use directions for rests
- understand and use directions for repeated bars
- understand and use directions for repeated chords
- condense a chord progression using repeat marks, 1st and 2nd time section endings, DS, DC and coda performance directions
- write out in full a chord progression that contains repeats, 1st and 2nd section endings, DS, DC and coda markings.

tempo

In popular music the most commonly used indication of tempo is to specify the *beats per minute* (*bpm*) – this is sometimes also referred to as the metronome marking.

For example: $\quad \downarrow = 60$

This means that there are 60 quarter note beats per minute.

For example: $\quad \downarrow = 120$

This means that there are 120 quarter note beats per minute, so a tempo of $\downarrow = 120$ bpm is twice as fast as a tempo of $\downarrow = 60$ bpm.

bpm can also be measured using other types of beat.

For example: $\quad \downarrow. = 60$

This means that there are 60 dotted quarter note beats per minute.

dynamics

Below are the symbols used to indicate how quietly or loudly the music should be played:

symbol	meaning	Italian term
pp	very softly	pianissimo
p	softly	piano
mp	moderately softly	mezzo piano
mf	moderately strongly	mezzo forte
f	strongly	forte
ff	very strongly	fortissimo

You can add more *p* s or *f* s to instruct the performer to play extremely quietly or loudly.

To indicate that the music should gradually become louder or quieter, *hairpins* are used.

This hairpin means that you should start quietly and gradually play louder.

Sometimes this is also indicated by the term *crescendo* (or *cresc.*).

This hairpin means that you should start loudly and gradually play more quietly.

Sometimes this is also indicated by the terms *decrescendo* (*decresc.*) or *diminuendo* (*dim.*).

To be really precise you should also indicate at which dynamic level you are starting and finishing. For example, the following direction means that you should start moderately loudly and gradually play more quietly, until you are playing very quietly by the end of the hairpin.

articulation

The following symbols tell you how to play each note.

A dot above or below the notehead tells you to play the note short – about half its length. This is known as a *staccato* dot.

A straight line above or below the notehead tells you to play the note for its full value and 'lean' on it slightly. This is known as a *tenuto* mark.

A 'V' lying on its side above or below a notehead means stress that note. This is called a (marcato) *accent*.

sfz is an abbreviation for sforzando which means 'forced' or accented. A *Sforzando* accent is more sharply stressed than a normal (marcato) accent. This is sometimes used in combination with a '*p*' (piano) and a 'hairpin'. The result is an accented note, reducing the volume immediately and then gradually

getting louder again. This type of articulation is often used in horn sections.

Slurs are used where notes should be played together as smoothly as possible. For example, saxophonists and brass instrumentalists will play all the slurred notes in one breath, without accenting any of them.

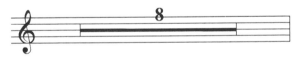

The symbol ⌒ is a *fermata* (although it is commonly known as a *pause* mark). It can be used with notes, chords or rests, and indicates that the note, chord or rest is held for an extra (unspecified) amount of time. The length of the *pause* is decided by the performer.

directions for rests

A bar of rest is indicated by a whole (semibreve) rest. If there is more than one bar of rest, a horizontal line is written through the bar with the number of silent bars written above it.

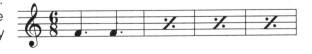

This is much easier for a performer to count than eight separate bars containing whole rests.

directions for repeats

- If one bar is to be repeated then the symbol ∕. can be used. This symbol can be repeated as necessary, although it is useful to the performer to re-write the actual phrase at the start of a new page.

For example:

If the phrase to be repeated is longer than one bar, a similar symbol is used but with two slanting lines crossing the same number of bars as in the phrase, and with the number of bars written above it.

For example:

Remember this means that two bars are to be repeated once, not one bar played twice.

- If a chord is to be repeated within a bar, the repeats can be indicated by oblique lines or dots.

For example:

| **C** / / / | **F** / / / | or | **C** . . . | **F** . . . |

This is very useful if there are two chords per bar and you wish to specify on which beat they change.

For example:

| **C** / / | **F** **G**₇ **C** / / ‖

If the rhythms are not specified then the performer will assume that the chord changes half-way through the bar.

- To indicate that a section of music should be repeated (played twice) *repeat marks* are used. A double bar-line, followed by two dots on either side of the middle line of the staff indicates the start of the section and two dots on either side of the middle line of the staff, followed by a double bar-line indicates the end of the section to be repeated. (If there are no dots at the start of the section, then repeat from the beginning of the piece).

Repeat marks can also be used for chord charts.

Any number of bars may be included within the repeat marks.

If the section is to be repeated more than once, the number of times it is to be played is written above the last repeat dots.

If two sections of music are identical, except for the last bar or bars, repeat marks are used in conjunction with *first time* and *second time* directions.

‖: **C** | **A**m7 | **D**m7 | **G**7 :‖ **D**m7 **G**7 | **C** |

There are two other standard directions for indicating that sections of the music are to be repeated:

1) *D.C.* (an abbreviation of *Da Capo*) means 'from the beginning'.

For example, if the entire piece of music is to be repeated, D.C. can be written at the end of the music and this instructs the performer to play it again from the beginning.

2) *D.S.* (an abbreviation of *Dal Segno*) means 'from the sign' (%).

For example, if the verse and chorus of a song are to be repeated, but not the introduction, D.S. can be written at the end of the music with the sign (%) written at the start of the verse. This instructs the performer to start again from the sign.

D.S. al Fine, means repeat from the sign (%) until the word *Fine* (which means 'end').

D.C. al Fine means repeat from the beginning until the word *Fine*.

A coda is the equivalent of an 'outro' (i.e. an ending section).

D.C. al Coda means repeat from the beginning and then 'play the coda'.

D.S. al Coda means repeat from the sign (%) and then 'play the coda'.

The symbol which is used to indicate from where in the repeat the performer should go to the coda is: ⊕

Usually some combination of repeat devices is required when writing out a chord chart or a piece of music. The general principle is to condense the information as much as possible whilst retaining clarity and avoiding page turns.

Example 1:

$$
\begin{array}{cccc}
| \quad C & | \quad F_{maj7} & | \quad D_m & | \quad G_7 \ C \ \| \text{(Fine)} \\
| \quad E_{m7} & | \quad A_{m7} & | \quad E_m & | \quad C \ G_7 \ \| \text{(D.C. al fine)}
\end{array}
$$

	C		F_{maj7}		D_m		G_7 C ‖ (Fine)

would be played as:

	C		F_{maj7}		D_m		G_7 C
E_{m7}		A_{m7}		E_m		C G_7
C		F_{maj7}		D_m		G_7 C ‖

Example 2:

%

| C | | F | | D_{m7} | | G | |

to Coda ⊕

| E_m | | G_7 | | C_{maj7} | | A_{m7} | |

D.S. al coda

| F | | G_7 | ‖ |

⊕
Coda | C | | F_6 | | G_7 | | C | ‖ |

would be played as:

C		F		D_{m7}		G	
E_m		G_7		C_{maj7}		A_{m7}	
F		G_7		D_{m7}		G	
E_m		G_7		C		F_6	
G_7		C	‖

The first question in this section of the exam will be as follows:

Q1. Write a brief essay, of approximately 200 to 300 words, describing the musical career of ONE musician or group of your choice from the list below.

In your essay include some information about:

a) the development of their musical career, including significant dates;

b) group members and the instruments played, or the groups/musicians the musician has played or recorded with;

c) recordings, including hit singles and albums.

The main focus of the essay should be on:

d) the main features of their music

e) an explanation of how their music was influenced by musicians from earlier periods

(*sample* list)

The Beatles	The Who	The Grateful Dead
Chuck Berry	Diana Ross	Stevie Wonder
Bob Dylan	The Doors	The Eagles
Eric Clapton		

Below are some examples of the other types of questions that candidates may be asked in this section of the exam. If you have difficulty answering any question, then carefully re-read the preceding chapter.

Q2. On the staff below, in drum notation, write one bar of the following (in $\frac{4}{4}$ time): bass (kick) drum on beats 1 and 3; snare drum on beats 2 and 4; hi hat on all 4 beats.

A2.

Q3. How do you transpose standard (concert) notation in order that an alto saxophone sounds at the same pitch as a non-transposing instrument (e.g. a keyboard)?

A3.

Q4. How would a performer play the following phrase?

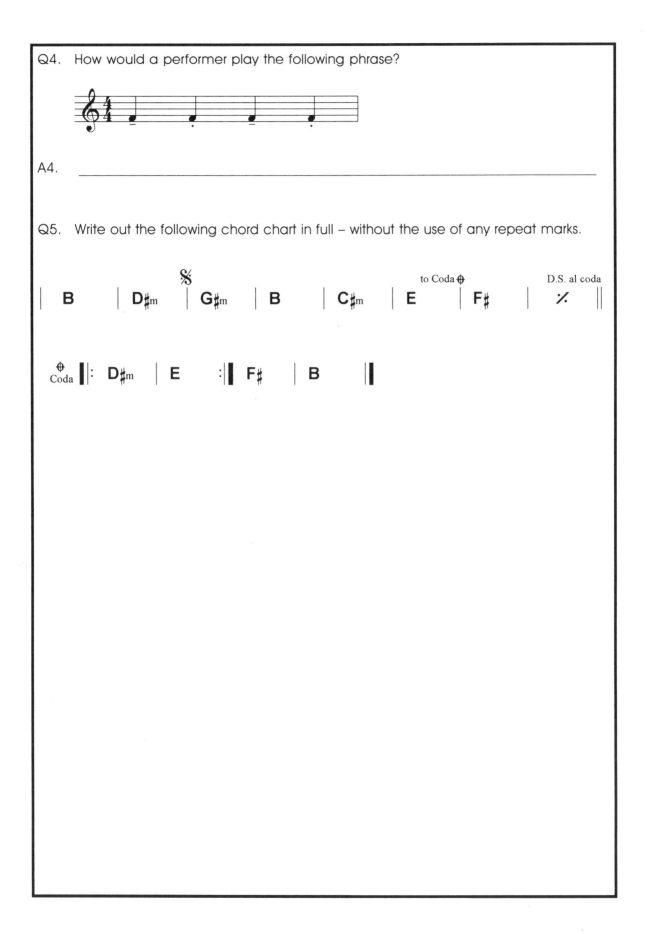

A4. _____

Q5. Write out the following chord chart in full – without the use of any repeat marks.

Section Five – harmony

In this section of the exam, within a range of keys up to four sharps and four flats you will be asked to demonstrate your knowledge of:

- the patterns of major 7th, minor 7th, dominant 7th and minor 7th ♭5 chords built from major and natural minor scales;

- dominant 7th chords from the harmonic minor scale;

- commonly occurring cadential chord movements;

- constructing chord progressions;

- the application of major, pentatonic major, natural minor, pentatonic minor and blues scales in improvisation.

So that the harmony learnt in theory can be used effectively in a practical way, you should be able to do the following:

- write out, and identify, the patterns of major 7th, minor 7th, dominant 7th and minor 7th ♭5 chords;

- write chord progressions in the keys listed, including using dominant 7th chords from the harmonic minor scale;

- identify and construct, commonly occurring cadential chord movements;

- identify which major, pentatonic major, natural minor, pentatonic minor or blues scales would be suitable to use for improvising over a given chord progression;

- write chord progressions over which major, pentatonic major, natural minor, pentatonic minor or blues scales could be used for improvising.

the theory

The type of seventh chord that can be built, by taking alternate notes, from each degree of a major scale is always the same for each particular scale degree, regardless of the key.

All major keys have the following pattern of chords:

I	II	III	IV	V	VI	VII
major 7th	minor 7th	minor 7th	major 7th	dominant 7th	minor 7th	minor 7th ♭5

Below are these chords built from the C, G, D, A, E, F, B♭, E♭ and A♭ major scales.

Degree:	I	II	III	IV	V	VI	VII
C major:	Cmaj7	Dm7	Em7	Fmaj7	G7	Am7	Bm7♭5
G major:	Gmaj7	Am7	Bm7	Cmaj7	D7	Em7	F#m7♭5
D major:	Dmaj7	Em7	F#m7	Gmaj7	A7	Bm7	C#m7♭5
A major:	Amaj7	Bm7	C#m7	Dmaj7	E7	F#m7	G#m7♭5
E major:	Emaj7	F#m7	G#m7	Amaj7	B7	C#m7	D#m7♭5
F major:	Fmaj7	Gm7	Am7	B♭maj7	C7	Dm7	Em7♭5
B♭ major:	B♭maj7	Cm7	Dm7	E♭maj7	F7	Gm7	Am7♭5
E♭ major:	E♭maj7	Fm7	Gm7	A♭maj7	B♭7	Cm7	Dm7♭5
A♭ major:	A♭maj7	B♭m7	Cm7	D♭maj7	E♭7	Fm7	Gm7♭5

Notice that the chords built on the 1st and 4th degrees are major 7th chords, the chords built on the 2nd, 3rd and 6th degrees are minor 7th chords, the chord built on the 5th degree is a dominant 7th chord and the chord built on the 7th degree is a minor 7th ♭5 chord.

The type of chord that can be built, by taking alternate notes, from each degree of a natural minor scale is always the same for each particular scale degree, regardless of the key.

All minor keys, based on the natural minor scale, have the following pattern of chords:

I	II	III	IV	V	VI	VII
minor 7th	minor 7th ♭5	major 7th	minor 7th	minor 7th	major 7th	dominant 7th

Below are these chords built from the A, E, B, F#, C#, D, G, C and F natural minor scales.

Degree:	I	II	III	IV	V	VI	VII
A minor:	Am7	Bm7♭5	Cmaj7	Dm7	Em7	Fmaj7	G7
E minor:	Em7	F#m7♭5	Gmaj7	Am7	Bm7	Cmaj7	D7
B minor:	Bm7	C#m7♭5	Dmaj7	Em7	F#m7	Gmaj7	A7
F# minor:	F#m7	G#m7♭5	Amaj7	Bm7	C#m7	Dmaj7	E7
C# minor:	C#m7	D#m7♭5	Emaj7	F#m7	G#m7	Amaj7	B7
D minor:	Dm7	Em7♭5	Fmaj7	Gm7	Am7	B♭maj7	C7
G minor:	Gm7	Am7♭5	B♭maj7	Cm7	Dm7	E♭maj7	F7
C minor:	Cm7	Dm7♭5	E♭maj7	Fm7	Gm7	A♭maj7	B♭7
F minor:	Fm7	Gm7♭5	A♭maj7	B♭m7	Cm7	D♭maj7	E♭7

Notice that the chords built on the 1st, 4th and 5th degrees are all minor 7th chords, the chords built on the 3rd and 6th degrees are major 7th chords, the chord built on the 7th degree is a dominant 7th chord and the chord built on the 2nd degree is a minor 7 ♭5th chord.

Degrees of the scale and the chords that are built on them, are traditionally, and still widely, identified using Roman numerals. This system provides a useful shortcut for writing chords, as it identifies the 'type' of chord as well as the 'position' of the chord in the scale. Below are the various seventh chords that are built from the C major and A natural minor scales identified using the Roman numeral system. By using the formulae below you can work out which seventh chords can be built from any major or natural minor scale.

C major	Chord:	Cmaj7	Dm7	Em7	Fmaj7	G7	Am7	Bm7♭5
	Roman numerals:	Imaj7	IIm7	IIIm7	IVmaj7	V7	VIm7	VIIm7♭5

A natural minor	Chord:	Am7	Bm7♭5	Cmaj7	Dm7	Em7	Fmaj7	G7
	Roman numerals:	Im7	IIm7♭5	♭IIImaj7	IVm7	Vm7	♭VImaj7	♭VII7

Below you will find a brief explanation as to why the chords from the natural minor scale are numbered in this way when using the Roman numeral system. In the exam, however, you will only be asked to identify, or write out the pattern of chords.

Supplementary explanation

The chords built from the natural minor scale are numbered in comparison to the chords built from the major scale with the same keynote. The flat sign before the chords built on the 3rd, 6th and 7th degrees indicates that the roots of these chords are one half step (semitone) lower than the roots of the corresponding chords built from the major scale with the same keynote. For example, in the key of C major the 3rd, 6th and 7th notes are E, A and B. In the scale of C natural minor the 3rd, 6th and 7th notes are E♭, A♭ and B♭. Therefore the roots of the chords built on these degrees of the C natural minor scale are all a half step lower than the roots of the chords built on same degrees of the C major scale.

Nashville numbering

Some musicians (particularly in the USA) prefer to use standard numbers in place of Roman numerals – this method of identifying chords is called the 'Nashville Numbering System'. An outline of this system of chord identification has been provided in the Grade Three book. In the exam, answers can be expressed using either system, providing you are consistent in your usage.

Technical names

Chords that occur on each degree of the scale have names that originate in classical music terminology. In popular music, only the three main chords of each key are still occasionally referred to by these names:

- The chord that occurs on the first degree of the scale is known as the *tonic*.
- The chord that occurs on the fourth degree of the scale is known as the *subdominant*.
- The chord that occurs on the fifth degree of the scale is known as the *dominant*.

6th chords

- Major 6th chords are extensions of major triads and can be used as alternatives to major triads or major seventh chords: in major keys they occur on the 1st , 4th and 5th degrees and are numbered I6, IV6 and V6 respectively. 6th chords can also be built from the 3rd, 6th and 7th degrees of the natural minor scale (♭III6, ♭VI6, ♭VII6).

- Minor 6th chords are extensions of minor triads and can be used as alternatives to minor seventh chords: in major keys, minor 6th chords can only be built diatonically (i.e. using notes from the key) on the 2nd degree of the scale and are numbered IIm6. Minor 6th chords can also be built from the 4th degree of the natural minor scale (IVm6).

Dominant 7th chords from the harmonic minor

The chord that is built, by taking four alternate notes, on the fifth degree of the harmonic minor scale is always a dominant 7th chord.

For example:

A harmonic minor	E dominant 7th
A B C D E F G♯ A	E G♯ B D

C♯ harmonic minor	G♯ dominant 7th
C♯ D♯ E F♯ G♯ A B♯ C♯	G♯ B♯ D♯ F♯

F harmonic minor	C dominant 7th
F G A♭ B♭ C D♭ E F	C E G B♭

This is a useful chord to use when writing chord progressions in minor keys. (This is explained further under 'cadences').

cadences

Historically, two cadences that have been used extensively both in classical and popular music are the *V – I cadence* (also called the *perfect cadence*) and the *IV – I cadence* (also called the *plagal cadence*).

The *V – I cadence* is the cadence which creates the strongest and most complete ending to a phrase. In the key of C major this can be played as either G to C, or G7 to C. By playing the V chord as a dominant 7th chord (rather than just a major triad) a stronger sounding cadence is created. Consequently, V – I cadences are often played as V7 – I.

The *IV – I cadence* is another cadence which is used to end a musical phrase although it is more subtle than a V – I cadence. In major keys the IV chord can be played both as a major triad or a major 7th chord, so the IV – I cadence in C major can be played as F to C or Fmaj7 to C.

In both cadences the I chord may also be played as a major seventh chord.

V – I cadences and IV – I cadences are also used in minor keys. The V – I cadence is the stronger and more final sounding cadence, whilst the IV – I cadence is more subtle. In progressions using chords built from the natural minor scale either minor triads or minor 7th chords can be used.

In order to create a stronger resolution, when using chords built from the natural minor scale, the V – I cadence often 'borrows' the fifth chord of the harmonic minor scale. The fifth chord of the harmonic minor scale is a dominant 7th chord which creates a greater sense of release when it resolves to the I chord, than if a minor 7th chord is used. Note, however, that the third of this chord is *non-diatonic* to the natural minor scale.

other cadential movements

In popular music there are no 'rules' about which chords should be used at particular points in a piece of music, however there are some combinations of chords which are often used to create *cadential movements* which can give the music structure and shape. Here are some of the most common cadential movements:

The V chord is often used as a temporary resting place during a piece of music, for example at the end of a verse before a chorus. In this cadence (which is traditionally known as the *imperfect cadence*) the V chord is usually approached by the I chord: in C major the cadence would be C to G, or C to G7.

The V chord is often followed by a chord other than the I chord. For example, the V chord is sometimes followed by the VI chord, (which is traditionally known as an *interrupted cadence*). In the key of C major this chord movement would be G to Em.

In progressions based on the natural minor scale the ♭VII or ♭VII7 chord is often used to lead back to the I chord – as this movement creates a sense of resolution. In the key of A minor this chord movement would be G (G7) to Am.

The most important factor regarding all of the above examples is how effective they sound in any particular piece of music. We recommend that, if possible, you play them on your instrument and experiment with them and other chord combinations when you are practising writing songs or chord progressions.

constructing chord progressions

There are many different approaches to writing chord progressions. The most important consideration is to decide how effective the chords sound in any particular combination. Here are a few tips on writing chord progressions that may be helpful:

- So that you can choose from the full range of chords, you need to know all the common chords that are in the key. You can work them out by using the formulae given previously.

- Starting the chord progression with the *tonic chord* will help to instantly define the pitch and tonality of the key.

- Using a V – I or IV – I cadence (in major and minor keys) or a ♭VII – I cadence (in a minor key) at the end of the progression will help to create a sense of 'reaching a resting point' or a feeling of 'arriving home'.

For example:

This A♭ major chord progression starts with the key chord and ends with a V – I cadence.

| A♭maj7 | C m7 F m7 | B♭m7 E♭7 | A♭maj7 |

This C# minor chord progression starts with the key chord and ends with a ♭VII – I cadence.

| C♯m7 | F♯m7 | A maj7 B 7 | C♯m7 |

Although both these progressions use cadences to effectively indicate the end of a musical phrase, it is not essential that phrases end in this way. When writing chord progressions, the most important consideration is *do the chords you have used create the musical effect you intended?*

Using chord variations

In order to achieve a wide variety of musical sounds, as well as 7th chords, you should consider using other chords that you have learnt at this grade and at lower grades when composing chord progressions:

- major or minor triads, and their inversions, can be used in place of major7th, minor 7th and dominant 7th chords.

- sus2 and sus4 triads can be used instead of (or resolving to) most major or minor triads. (However, a sus4 triad based on the 4th degree of the major scale, and a sus2 triad based on the 5th degree of the natural minor scale, will both involve a non-diatonic note).

- depending upon the style, 5th 'power chords' can be used in place of major and minor triads.

- Major 6th and minor 6th chords can be used as described earlier in this chapter.

Candidates are not expected to be fluent in using (non-diatonic) diminished 7th chords in composition at this grade.

writing blues

The harmony used in blues-based music falls outside standard musical harmony. The chords in blues-based music are normally dominant 7ths (i.e. extensions of major triads), but melodies and improvisations are often based on the blues scale which can be seen as a variation of the pentatonic minor scale. It is the clash and dissonance between these two key types that gives blues music its distinctive sound.

There are no 'rules' in writing blues-based chord progressions, but the chords that are often used are dominant 7th chords built on the 1st, 4th and 5th degrees of the scale, although a variety of other chords can occur according to different stylistic traditions. For example, in a blues-based chord progression in C, the chords that are often used are C7, F7 and G7. However, the A♭, B♭ and E♭ triads also commonly occur and, if the music is stylistically in the rock tradition, 5th 'power chords' are often used.

improvisation

Major and pentatonic major scales are used for improvising in major keys. For example, if a chord progression uses chords from the key of E major, then the E major or E pentatonic major scale would be an appropriate scale to use for improvising.

Natural minor and pentatonic minor scales are used for improvising in minor keys. For example, if a chord progression uses chords from the key of C# minor, then the C# natural minor or C# pentatonic minor scale would normally be an appropriate scale to use for improvising.

Blues scales are the main scales used for improvising over blues-based chord progressions. The chords used to accompany this scale are normally dominant 7th chords, although other chord types can also be used.

scale choices

The most reliable method of deciding which scale to use over a chord progression is to first analyse the chords to assess which key they belong to.

Because the chords built from any major scale and its relative minor are the same, it is important to look at how the chord progression is structured in order to correctly identify the

key. Normally, a chord progression will start and finish on the I (tonic) chord, and this will indicate whether the progression is in the major or relative minor key.

Blues keys can be recognised by their reliance on dominant 7th chords on the 1st, 4th and 5th degrees of the scale, as well as other non-diatonic chords.

For example, C blues scale would fit over any combination of C7, F7, G7, A♭, B♭ & E♭.

Here are examples of chord progressions in major, minor and blues keys.

Sample chord progression in E major:

Emaj7	**G♯**m7 **C♯**m7	**A**maj7 **B**7	**E**maj7
Imaj7	IIIm7 VIm7	IVmaj7 V7	Imaj7

The E major scale or the E pentatonic major scale would be good scale choices for improvisation.

Sample chord progression in C# minor:

C♯m7	**B** **A**maj7	**F♯**m7 **G♯**m7	**C♯**m7
Im7	♭VII ♭VImaj7	IVm7 Vm7	Im7

The C# natural minor scale or the C# pentatonic minor scale would be good scale choices for improvisation.

Sample blues-based chord progression in C:

C7	**F**7	**A♭** **G**7	**C**7
I7	IV7	♭VI V7	I7

The C blues scale would be a good scale choice for improvisation.

When you are writing a chord progression to be used as a backing for improvisation the same process as described above applies. For major and minor keys work out the possible chords that can built on each degree of that scale, and then experiment with different possible combinations until you come up with some progressions that you like. Remember that using a V-I or IV-I cadence (in major and minor keys) or a ♭VII-I cadence (in minor keys) is a straightforward and effective way to create an ending to a progression.

For blues-based progressions work out the dominant 7th chords on the 1st, 4th and 5th degrees. For other chord options an investigation into different stylistic traditions is necessary as there are no fixed 'rules'.

Below are some examples of the types of questions that candidates may be asked in this section of the exam. If you can't answer a question, then carefully re-read the preceding chapter and, if necessary, refer to the earlier books in the series.

Q1. Using chord symbols, write out the 7th chords that are built from each degree of the A♭ major scale.

A1. _____

Q2. Using chord symbols, write out the 7th chords that are built from each degree of the C# natural minor scale.

A2. _____

Q3. Identify the cadences which are created between:

(a) the two chords in bar 2

(b) the 2nd chord in bar 3 and the chord in bar 4.

| E F#m7 | B7 C#m7 | G#m7 A | E |

A3. a) _____

b) _____

Q4. Using at least three different chords, write a four bar chord progression in the key of F minor with the last two chords forming a ♭VII – I cadence.

A4. | | | | ||

Q5. Name a scale that could be used effectively for improvising over the following chord progression.

| A♭7 | D♭7 | E E♭7 | A♭7 |

A5. _____

Q6. Using at least three different chords, write a four bar chord progression over which the F# pentatonic minor scale could be used for improvisation.

A6. | | | | ||

Section Six – transposition

In this section of the exam you will be asked to demonstrate your skills in transposing chord progressions. You will be asked to transpose a chord progression into any key within a range of keys up to four sharps or four flats.

the theory

There are two different methods that you can use to transpose chord progressions. Both methods will give exactly the same result.

chord numbers

Identify the key of the original chord progression and the chord numbers for each of the chords. Next, using the chord numbers, work out the chords in the new key.

For example, to transpose the following chord progression into the key of G major, the first step is to identify the key of the progression.

| E_{maj7} | $C\sharp_{m7}$ $F\sharp_{m7}$ | B_7 | E_{maj7} |

The above chord progression is in the key of E major because:

- the progression starts and ends on an E major 7th chord.

- all the chords are in the key of E major.

- the movement of B7 to Emaj7 forms a V-I (perfect cadence) in the key of E major

Having worked out the key of the progression, identify the key chord – which would have the chord number 'I'. From this, the other chord numbers can then be worked out. You can check that you have worked them out correctly by ensuring that the chord type for each degree corresponds to the standard major scale pattern of triads and chords.

The chord numbers for the above progression are:

| Imaj7 | VIm7 IIm7 | V7 | Imaj7 |

To transpose the chord progression into G major, you need to work out what the Imaj7,

VIm7, IIm7, and V7 chords are, in the key of G major. Remember, the chord types remain the same as in the original key – therefore the chord progression transposed into the key of G major will be:

| G_{maj7} | E_{m7} A_{m7} | D_7 | G_{maj7} |

The same principle applies when transposing between two minor keys, the only difference being that chords should be numbered according to their position in the pattern of chords built from the minor scale.

intervals

Identify the key of the original chord progression (as described above). Next, identify the interval between the keynotes of the original key and the new key. This will determine the interval you need to move each chord (either up or down). In this instance, G is a minor 3rd above E, so for this transposition, the root note of each chord needs to be moved up a minor third or three half steps. As with the previous method, the chord types stay the same as in the original key.

- Emaj7 would move up a minor 3rd to Gmaj7.

- C#m7 would move up a minor 3rd to Em7.

- F#m7 would move up a minor 3rd to Am7.

- B7 would move up a minor 3rd to D7.

The same method can be used to transpose between two minor keys.

Below are some examples of the types of questions that candidates may be asked in this section of the exam. If you can't answer a question, then carefully re-read the preceding chapter. Once you've worked through these questions you can check your answers by looking in the back of the book.

Q1. Transpose the following chord progression into the key of C minor.

| **F**m | **D**♭ **B**♭m7 | **G**m7♭5 **C**7 | **F**m |

A1. | | | | |

Q2. Transpose the following chord progression into the key of E♭ major.

| **A** | **C**♯m7 | **F**♯m7 **B**m7 | **E**7 **A**maj7 |

A2. | | | | |

Section Seven – sample answers

Note that all the answers below are 'sample answers' and for several questions there are a range of other answers that would also be acceptable.

Section One – scales and keys   [Max. 20 marks]

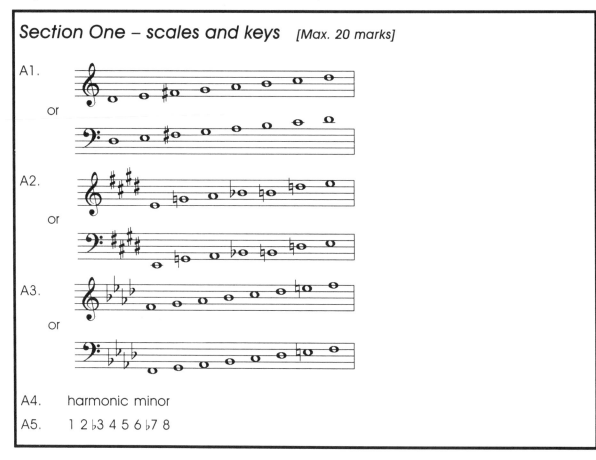

A1.   or

A2.   or

A3.   or

A4.   harmonic minor

A5.   1 2 ♭3 4 5 6 ♭7 8

Section Two – chords   [Max. 20 marks]

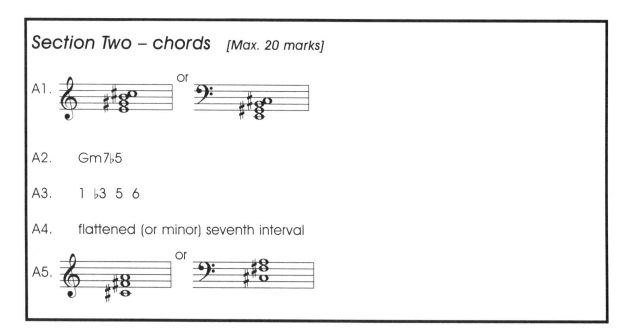

A1.   or

A2.   Gm7♭5

A3.   1 ♭3 5 6

A4.   flattened (or minor) seventh interval

A5.   or

Section Three – rhythm notation [Max. 10 marks]

A1.
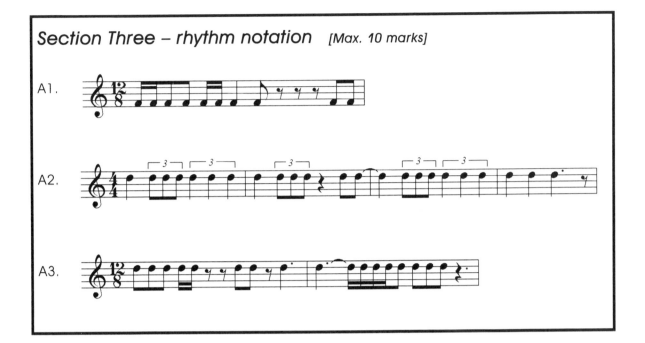

A2.

A3.

Section Four – knowledge of popular music [Max. 15 marks]

A1. An essay describing the musical career of a musician or group from the list given in Section Four.

A2.
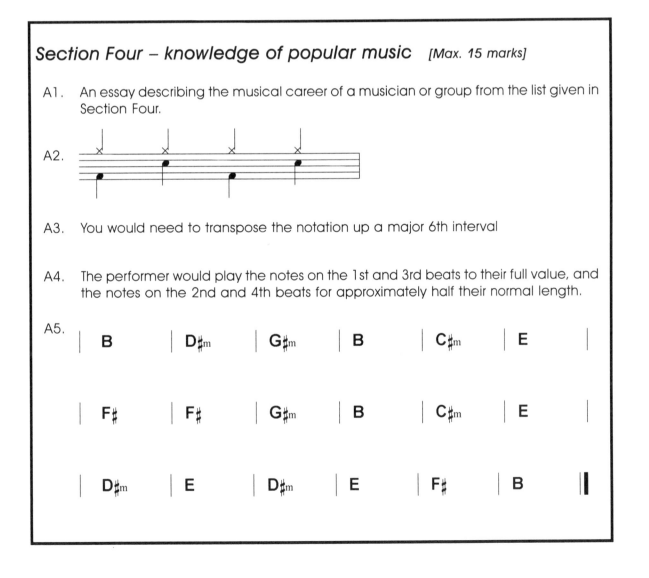

A3. You would need to transpose the notation up a major 6th interval

A4. The performer would play the notes on the 1st and 3rd beats to their full value, and the notes on the 2nd and 4th beats for approximately half their normal length.

A5.

| B | D♯m | G♯m | B | C♯m | E | |

| F♯ | F♯ | G♯m | B | C♯m | E | |

| D♯m | E | D♯m | E | F♯ | B | |

Section Five – harmony   *[Max. 25 marks]*

A1.   A♭maj7 B♭m7 Cm7 D♭maj7 E♭7 Fm7 Gm7♭5

A2.   C#m7 D#m7♭5 Emaj7 F#m7 G#m7 Amaj7 B7

A3.   a) V7 – VIm7 (interrupted cadence)
       b) IV – I (plagal cadence)

A4.
Fm7	**D**♭maj7	**E**♭	**F**m

A5.   A♭ blues scale

A6.
F♯m7	**B**m7	**C**♯m7	**E** **F**♯m7

Section Six – transposition   *[Max. 10 marks]*

A1.
Cm	**A**♭ **F**m7	**D**m7♭5 **G**7	**C**m

A2.
E♭	**G**m7	**C**m7 **F**m7	**B**♭7 **E**♭maj7

Examination Entry Form for LCM
Popular Music Theory examination.

GRADE FIVE

PLEASE COMPLETE CLEARLY USING BLOCK CAPITAL LETTERS

SESSION (Summer/Winter): _____ YEAR: _____

Preferred Examination Centre (if known): _____

If left blank, you will be examined at the nearest examination centre to your home address.

Candidate Details:

Candidate Name (as to appear on certificate):

_____

Address: _____

_____

_____ Postcode: _____

Tel. No. (day): _____ (evening): _____

Teacher Details:

Teacher Name (as to appear on certificate): _____

Registry Tutor Code (if applicable): _____

Address: _____

_____ Postcode: _____

Tel. No. (day): _____ (evening): _____

IMPORTANT NOTES

- It is the candidate's responsibility to have knowledge of, and comply with, the current syllabus requirements. Where candidates are entered for examinations by teachers, the teacher must take responsibility that candidates are entered in accordance with the current syllabus requirements. In particular, from 2005 it is important to check that the contents of this book match the syllabus that is valid at the time of entry.

- For candidates with special needs, a letter giving details should be attached.

- Theory dates are the same worldwide and are fixed annually by LCM. Details of entry deadlines and examination dates are obtainable from the Examinations Registry.

- Submission of this entry is an undertaking to abide by the current regulations as listed in the current syllabus and any subsequent regulations updates published by the LCM / Examinations Registry.

- UK entries should be sent to The Examinations Registry, Registry House, Churchill Mews, Dennett Rd, Croydon, Surrey CR0 3JH.

- Overseas entrants should contact the LCM / Examinations Registry for details of their international representatives.

Examination Fee   £ _____

Late Entry Fee (if applicable)   £ _____

Total amount submitted: £ _____

Cheques or postal orders should be made payable to The Examinations Registry.
Entries cannot be made by credit card.

A current list of fees is available from the Examinations Registry.

The Examinations Registry
Registry House
Churchill Mews
Dennett Road
Croydon
Surrey, U.K.
CR0 3JH

Tel: 020 8665 7666
Fax: 020 8665 7667
Email: mail@ExamRegistry.com